WISE
LEADERSHIP

WISE
LEADERSHIP

Linda A. McLyman

Michigan State University Press • *East Lansing*

♾ The paper used in this publication meets the minimum requirements of ANSI/NISO
Z39.48-1992 (R 1997) (Permanence of Paper).

 Michigan State University Press
East Lansing, Michigan 48823-5245

Printed and bound in the United States of America.

11 10 09 08 07 06 05   1 2 3 4 5 6 7 8 9 10

LIBRARY OF CONGRESS CATALOGING-IN-PUBLICATION DATA
McLyman, Linda A.
Wise leadership / Linda A. McLyman.
p. cm.
ISBN 0-87013-746-8 (alk. paper)
1. Leadership. I. Title.
HD57.7.M398 2005
658.4'092—dc22
2005003509

Cover design by Heather Truelove Aiston
Book design by Sharp Des!gns, Inc., Lansing, MI

green press INITIATIVE   Michigan State University Press is a member of the Green Press Initiative
and is committed to developing and encouraging ecologically responsible
publishing practices. For more information about the Green Press Initiative and the use
of recycled paper in book publishing, please visit *www.greenpressinitiative.com*.

Visit Michigan State University Press on the World Wide Web at *www.msupress.msu.edu*

CONTENTS

for Daniel, Charles, and Marilyn

ACKNOWLEDGMENTS

I WANT TO TAKE THIS OPPORTUNITY TO THANK THE people in my life who have helped make this book become a reality. First, and most important, my deepest gratitude is extended to my beloved husband (and business partner) Daniel Leete. Your constant belief in me and my creative passions speaks volumes to me about your endless spirit of love, and optimism. You are a creative genius in your own right, and I respect you immensely. Thank you for the endless shared lessons, our partnership, and for the constant support you gave me while I was writing this book. You are one of the wisest leaders I know, and your contribution to both this book and our professional leadership work means a great deal to me and to others. I guess the old sign on the wall in our back room says it all: *"We make a great team!"*

I also want to thank the multitude of clients and colleagues who have helped shape both this book and my professional life. I cannot begin to thank you enough for providing the fuel for my learning and for my commitment toward developing better leaders. Although I have not specifically named you, you know who you are and you know how much you mean to me. Again, my deep-felt thanks.

I would be remiss in not mentioning the teachers who have helped me on my own path toward wise leadership. A special thanks to Gail Straub, David Gershon, and my fellow friends and colleagues in the GRACE training group. We have had a great ride together during the past decade. I am also indebted to the late Virginia Satir for all her wisdom and teaching.

I want to extend a special thanks to Julie Loehr, Julie Reaume, Kristine Blakeslee, and Annette Tanner at MSU Press. I appreciate all you have done to make this book work and also for holding my hand as a new author. I am grateful for your help and continual patience.

Lastly, thank you to my parents Charles and Marilyn McLyman. You instilled in me the love of life at a very young age and for that I am eternally grateful.

INTRODUCTION

THE PERSONAL JOURNEY TOWARD BECOMING a wise leader is a very important journey. At this point in history our world needs leaders who are willing to make a sincere commitment to individual growth and development. We need men and women who will take the time and energy to broaden their consciousness—in essence, heighten their awareness about who they are and how they operate in relationship to the people they influence and lead. Although it may not be realistic to expect our leaders to walk the path of full enlightenment, we need leaders who will make the commitment to becoming more fully conscious and awake. Our societies are crying out for leaders who are willing to create the kinds of relationships and partnerships that will build better businesses, better organizations, better families, and ultimately a better world. We need leaders who will continue to be willing to learn more about themselves and the world at large at every opportunity. We also need leaders who are willing to invest the time and energy needed in order to learn to make highly responsible, yet nonreactive choices and decisions. It is time for our workplaces and our societies to do whatever it takes to develop wise leaders. We need to do this for many reasons; perhaps the most important of these is the need to build a safer and more sustainable planet. My hope is that people from all walks of life will continue to work together to make this an attainable vision.

Leadership development is demanding. Sincere growth or development of any kind requires tremendous stamina and determination. It exacts a great deal of commitment and discipline from the individual. In essence, the task itself asks us to work diligently to broaden our views and to deepen our consciousness on all levels.

In recent years corporate America has spent a great deal of time, money, and energy developing bright, intelligent leaders. The time has come to make this same investment in cultivating emotionally mature, highly principled, more fully aware, and ultimately wiser leaders. It will be challenging to find ways to do this. The quest for attaining maturity and wisdom can be rigorous. Wisdom is not something that can necessarily be taught. Maturity is not necessarily a byproduct of aging. In much of our American society we value technological growth and intellectual development much more highly than we value personal growth and emotional development. Although the challenge to develop wise leaders requires a great deal of risk taking and experimentation, I believe the time is ripe to set the context for cultivating more maturity and more wisdom in our communities and in our work settings. We need to find the patience, the creativity, and courage to do just that.

In my twenty-plus years as a corporate teacher and management consultant I have had the good fortune to work alongside many gifted, emotionally mature, and wise people. I refer to these stellar individuals as my "learning partners." I have had the opportunity to learn from and also to teach many fine leaders. It has been a privilege to do this type of work.

My purpose in writing this book is to share some of what I have learned about wise and mature leadership. I hope the insights I have gained will encourage and inspire you to continue on your own path of self-discovery. I have always believed that as the individual develops and grows, the organization, the family, and the community he or she is part of grows as well. I suspect that anyone reading this book believes in the path of wisdom. I wish you the very best on your own journey.

THE UNIVERSALS

For many years I have been intrigued by observing the ways in which people do, or do not, lead others successfully. The most gifted leaders I have worked with represent a diversity of people from all walks of life. Although these leaders differ in terms of age, sex, race, religious beliefs, values, and job experiences, I have found that many of these individuals seem to think and respond to the world in ways that are more similar than not. Perhaps this is because wise and mature leaders really believe that all people are connected to each other at the deepest level. Wise leaders seek not only to accomplish and do, but also to aim their accomplishing and doing toward a goal of creating a better world.

At a time when so many people are feeling jaded and hopeless about the mass amount of destruction and violence that is happening in the world, any statement about leaders attempting to create a better world may sound trite. As I look closely at the wisest people I have worked with I am reminded, nevertheless, that these leaders do not care if people poke fun at their altruistic motives. Wise leaders are wholeheartedly committed to being responsible for creating better environments in which others can prosper and grow. Wise leaders, I have found, care deeply about the future of the planet and the future of their fellow human beings.

During the past twenty years of my career I have made it my business to learn as much as I can about the principles and practices that underlie wise leadership. People who lead wisely demonstrate some universal behaviors. At both the beginning and the end of this short book I have listed the principles and practices that I believe underlie wise leadership. At first glance the principles and practices may seem simple or obvious. I encourage you as the reader, however, to think deeply about what I have written. I think you will find that these principles and practices are indeed more complex than they may appear to be at a first glance.

In the main text of this book you will find short excerpts that highlight examples of the ways in which many of the leaders I have worked with think, act, and respond. If you do not want to read this book from beginning to end, I encourage you to jump in and start reading anywhere that piques your interest. You can gain insight about wise leadership by simply reading the text in any order.

I hope you will not view the content of this book to be prescriptive in nature. The book is not meant to be a "how to" book on leadership, but rather more of a platform to help you create your own path for develop-ment and growth as a leader. Though sometimes it stunts our growth to compare or contrast ourselves with others, other times this comparison actually is helpful. If we are willing to stay open without a great deal of self-judgment, we can learn from others in myriad ways.

My own commitment to learning, growing, changing, and gaining more self-acceptance as an individual has been highly influenced by working, studying, and living alongside other people who want to continue to practice wise leadership. I welcome any thoughts or ideas you may have about creating a path toward wise leadership. It is an exciting journey, please join me at any juncture of your own path.

UNIVERSAL BEHAVIORS
UNDERLYING WISE LEADERSHIP

- *Wise leaders continuously pursue growth and development as a form of lifelong learning.*

Wise leaders never stop learning about themselves, others, or the world in which they live. They want to continue to grow because they care deeply about their own future and the future of the planet. Wise leaders are wholeheartedly committed to being responsible for creating better environments in which people can prosper and grow.

- *Wise leaders are very creative and visionary in their approach toward life.*

Wise leaders seek to create and set visions at every possible opportunity. Wise leaders are much more visionary and proactive, than problem-oriented and reactive. Wise leaders spend more time focusing on what they want to accomplish and do, and much less time focusing on what is wrong.

- *Wise leaders have a keen awareness about their place in the bigger scheme of things. They combine a big passion and a big purpose with a "right-sized" ego.*

Wise leaders know when to step forward and when to step back. They have integrated the difficult life lessons regarding ego, power, and control. Wise leaders have learned to relax, and yet they remain committed to moving forward in order to accomplish their goals.

■ *Wise leaders have exceptional relationship and communication skills. They find human connections to be deeply satisfying.*

Wise leaders have an astute understanding about people. They comprehend the universal behaviors that make all human beings tick. Wise leaders understand how to create ideas and solutions with other human beings. Wise leaders seek to enhance the ways in which people can harmoniously live, work, and create together.

■ *Wise leaders lead with a strong sense of authenticity and integrity.*

Wise leaders have a strong commitment to their personal value system, and they demonstrate this in the action steps they take when leading others. Wise leaders are highly committed, responsible human beings. They are not afraid to make very difficult decisions.

- *Wise leaders demonstrate a high degree of emotional maturity.*

Wise leaders have learned to tolerate the kinds of emotional upheaval that other people frequently find too difficult to handle. Wise leaders do not flee from difficult situations or difficult feelings. Wise leaders can handle chaotic or painful situations without needing to apply quick fix strategies or solutions.

- *Wise leaders aim to embrace balance in their lives.*

Wise leaders realize that attaining physical, emotional and spiritual balance in all aspects of their lives is a requirement for gathering more wisdom. They seek to renew themselves on a daily basis. Wise leaders develop practices for attaining balance in their lives and apply discipline in order to utilize these practices.

- *Wise leaders are compassionate human beings.*

Wise leaders work hard to bring out the best in themselves and other people. They inspire others to do the same. Wise leaders do not shy away from being viewed as fun loving, enthusiastic, caring, or even deeply loving human beings. Wise leaders understand how to care about people without aiming to take care of them.

Wise leaders continuously pursue growth and development as a form of lifelong learning.

Wise leaders never stop learning about themselves, others, or the world in which they live. They want to continue to grow because they care deeply about their own future and the future of the planet. Wise leaders are wholeheartedly committed to being responsible for creating better environments in which people can prosper and grow. ■

- The wisest leaders I have known are lifelong learners. They allow others to teach them. In fact, they relish being the student.

- Life, for the wise leader, is simply a series of exciting learning opportunities.

- Wise leaders continuously pursue growth and development as a form of lifelong learning. They teach others to see life as one big experiment.

- Wise leaders have learned that growth is nonlinear. They expect to encounter the same difficult lessons over and over again but with deeper and more profound insight each time.

- Mature leaders do not view the world through the simplistic lens of how many wins or gains they can accrue. Wise leaders know that there is much more to life than tallying their successes and their failures.

- Corporate T-shirt slogans rarely change people or organizational behavior. Real growth and change require much more diligence. Wise leaders never invest in hype.

- Wise leaders know themselves well, and yet they continuously ask themselves "Who am I?" "What do I really stand for?" "What am I doing with my life?"

■ Wise leaders understand the
  reciprocal relationship between
  growing the individual and
  growing the organization. As
  the individual matures and
  grows, the organization matures
  and grows. As the organization
  matures and grows, the
  individual matures and grows.

■ How do we really encourage
  growth and maturity in our
  agencies, specifically in our
  leaders? Some of the wisest
  people I know are wrestling with
  this question.

- A mature leader deals with his or her fears wisely. He or she knows that facing one's fears directly provides a forum for continuous growth. A wise leader nevertheless is not afraid to seek help when he or she feels anxious or vulnerable. A mature leader often turns to a coach, therapist, mentor, advisor, or spiritual teacher for help when he or she is riddled by too much fear.

- I was asked to coach a woman who heads a large insurance company. Mary Lou has a reputation for being an exceptional leader. During our first meeting, I asked Mary Lou why people actually competed for the opportunity to work under her leadership. Quietly, Mary Lou answered, "I expect everyone to perform well for me, but I also consider everyone to be my learning partner."

- When learning and growth are nonhierarchal, everyone benefits.

- How can we develop, change, and grow as leaders without turning ourselves into constant self-improvement projects? A mature leader will be willing to wrestle with this complex question.

- I am often asked if growth is ever easy or pain-free. I do not believe that all growth has to be difficult or painful. Most wise people I have worked with nevertheless have told me to expect to encounter a lot of pain, confusion, and struggle along the path.

- Risks offer us the opportunity to grow. This is *always* true.

- My business partner regularly reminds me that some people take their risk in security and others take their security in risk.

■ Experienced leaders never deny
that stages of chaos are a natural
part of all change and growth
cycles. Experienced leaders
accept the reality that all human
beings experience varying
degrees of anxiety when they
move through stages of
transition. Wise individuals
know they, themselves, are not
immune to feeling resistance
and fear when they experience
difficult transitions.

- Mature leaders recognize the difference between true organizational change and crisis management.

- When people are not given ample opportunity to integrate the emotional experiences that accompany difficult growth and change they often feel drained and exhausted for extended periods of time.

■ A very wise woman approached her last twelve weeks of life with a complete sense of reverence and awe for what she was able to learn about herself as she faced her own death. She often spoke about how much she was able to grow during her last weeks. I was astonished by her openness to learning, especially when her physical and emotional suffering was so acute.

- Most organizations shy away from really growing their people. Wise leaders, however, spend time, money, and energy investing in the development of their people. They seek to grow their people in every way possible.

- Wise leaders understand the importance of continued individual growth (in contrast to narcissistic self-improvement) at the core level of their being.

*W*ise leaders are very creative
and visionary in their approach
toward life.

*W*ise leaders seek to create and set visions at every possible opportunity. Wise leaders are much more visionary and proactive than problem-oriented and reactive. Wise leaders spend more time focusing on what they want to accomplish and do and much less time focusing on what is wrong. ■

- Mature leadership is about creating and realizing visions, not about solving small problems. Wise leaders focus most of their energy on what they want to accomplish, manifest, or create. They focus very little of their energy on what they want to dismantle or fix.

- A wise leader sets the intention for an intelligent and attainable vision and then gets out of the way so real progress can take place.

- Mature leaders do not focus on dysfunction. New science teaches us that what we focus on most keenly is what we help to create.

- Any professional who has been trained to be an expert linear or analytical thinker can get very conditioned in either/or–type thinking. Either/or–type thinking is comforting. It gives us the illusion of being in control. It is also very limiting and dangerous at times. A mature leader watches for the trap of either/or–type thinking.

- A mature leader is not afraid to widen his or her worldview.

- I love the theory of "and." It reduces our reliance on "but" thinking.

- People view so much of what they discuss at work through the lens of, "What do we need to correct, change, or fix?" There is nothing wrong with fixing problems. However, if we rely on the use of the "fix it" model too strongly, we stifle our creativity and limit our ability to see the bigger picture. Leaders need to let go of their need to always be fixing problems.

- In the name of recreating, re-engineering, replacing, and repackaging ourselves, have we begun to think of ourselves and our organizations as a box of broken parts?

- Mature leaders do not fall into the trap of using too much analysis. It is seductive to analyze everything because doing so often gives us the illusion of being right or being in control. We all need to be able to use good analytical skills. However, we need to learn to recognize when we have overused our analytical muscles.

- Mature leaders have learned
  that the constant need to fix
  something is a subtle trap set
  by the ego.

- Curiosity opens us up. The most
  innovative and creative leaders
  I have worked with are very
  curious human beings.

- Good team leaders seldom fall into the trap of letting people spend too much time talking about what is going wrong. A mature leader always notices this behavior and subtlety shifts his or her team away from the topic of what isn't working and toward the question "What is it that we most want to do or accomplish?" This subtle shift makes a huge difference in how a team solves problems.

- Wise leaders understand the relationship between desire, vision and solid intention.

- Stop editing. Keep creating!

- Wise leaders know when to turn their attention toward the task of creation. They know that certain forms of editing are really covers for insecurity and fear.

- We have all been conditioned in outdated Newtonian-style thinking. Therefore, we have learned to solve problems from an outdated model. Wise leaders recognize this error.

- Each time a leadership team revisits a major decision, they make one less decision.

- When teams are too risk-aversive in their decision-making process people feel safe, yet somewhat bored. When teams learn to create and become comfortable with risky solutions they often feel much more excited and enlivened by their choices.

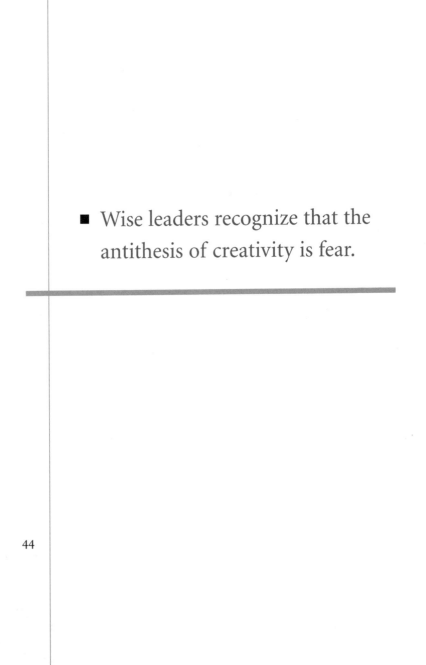

■ Wise leaders recognize that the antithesis of creativity is fear.

- Here is a recommendation I often give to executive teams:

  "At today's meeting I suggest we stop being so critical and corrective. Instead of engaging in all the 'I'm rights' and 'you're wrongs,' let's be a bit more creative and visionary."

  This is not a silly exercise; mature leaders do not allow people to waste time strutting their egos.

- In some levels of modern American society (even in corporate America), it has become popular to try to "cure our dysfunction." We want to analyze, label, fix, heal, and weed out all the things we consider to be wrong with ourselves or our organizations. In fact, many of us have inadvertently become "dysfunction experts." Interestingly enough, the more time and energy we focus on dysfunction, the less progress we actually make.

- The anthropologist in me knows how to simply observe and note behavior without recording any judgment. The analyst in me knows how to judge and criticize. Leaders often need to condition themselves to observe rather than judge. When leaders analyze too quickly they often arrive at poor decisions.

- We are all much more creative than we realize. We do not need to learn to be creative. Instead, we need to learn ways to unleash our inherent and natural creativity.

- A mature leader always provides an environment where people are free to innovate and create without fear of punishment. Most leaders say they are going to do just that, but very few actually do.

- Tom told his executive team they were going to take the time to seriously look at their strategic goals. He admitted that no one in the firm had a clear sense of where the agency was heading or what the top priorities were. Interestingly, Tom also noted that everyone who worked for him had a tremendous amount of work to do. What Tom's team needed to do was to find the time and energy to decide if the right work was getting done. Highly visionary leaders force their teams to commit to real strategic work.

- Wise leaders do not think of creativity as something as simple as inherent talent or learned skill. They view creativity as immense energy manifesting within and through each person.

- Remember that the words *relate* and *create* rhyme!

- Wise leaders view all human beings as inherently resourceful and creative. They believe in the vast potential of themselves and other human beings.

- Wise leaders have discovered the wonderful relationship between creativity and hope.

*W*ise leaders have a keen awareness about their place in the bigger scheme of things. They combine a big passion with a "right-sized" ego.

*W*ise leaders know when to step forward and when to step back. They have integrated the difficult life lessons regarding ego, power, and control. Wise leaders have learned to relax, and yet they remain committed to moving forward in order to accomplish their goals. ■

- Wise leaders have integrated the difficult life lessons regarding ego, power, and control. They have learned to accept what they can control and also what they can not control—in other words, they know when and how to let go.

- Wise leaders are often very passionate people, yet they seem to have a lighthearted presence or attitude. They can—and often do—laugh at themselves easily.

- Leadership is very important. However, when we confuse doing important work with being important, we tend to make a big mess of things. The most mature and wisest leaders I have known have had the ability to laugh at themselves while still accomplishing a lot of great things. They know how to engage in serious business without taking themselves too seriously.

- A leader has to first develop a solid sense of self in order to learn to let go of his or her need to be seen in center stage all of the time. Most of us make many mistakes before we really learn this lesson.

- Wise leaders rarely confuse arrogance with confidence.

- During times of change and transition, a mature leader is not afraid to temporarily add more structure to any given situation. He or she will intuitively know when to let go of any temporary or unnecessary structure.

- *Insistence*

  Persistence

  Resistance

  Interestingly, these words rhyme.

- Wise leaders do not confuse insistence with determination.

- Wise leaders know when to
  offer advice to others and when
  to say nothing at all.

- At the end of each day, ask
  yourself why you did or did not
  offer people advice that day.
  The leaders who have done this
  exercise tell me it shifts the whole
  way they approach leadership.

- Poor leadership leaves a lasting impression. In fact, people spend a lot of time complaining about the oppressive or difficult leaders they have worked for. A mature leader knows it takes a while for people to let go of the negative residue that a poor leader leaves behind. Sometimes "psychic burial" is truly needed.

■ A new leader told me that he saw himself as funny, motivating, and charismatic. His staff told me that he was loud, self-centered, and demanded a great deal of attention. Who do you think was most accurate in their description?

- My first mentor was an incredibly bright and wise woman. One day, after listening to me talk on the phone with an important client, she asked me this thought-provoking question: "Why is it that so many of you young people need to prove how smart you are?"

■ "I love working with him," Paul told me. "His presence just seems to fill up the room." Impressed, I asked, "Did his predecessor have the same impact on people?" "No," Paul laughed. "When his predecessor entered the room, he simply took up too much space."

- Strong decision makers use a variety of decision-making styles. Strong decision makers know when to, and when not to, share power. A strong decision maker is not afraid to step up to the plate when other people are reluctant or unwilling to make a difficult decision. A strong decision maker is also willing to share decision-making space when the context is right to do so.

- "If you have any guts," she bellowed, "you'll tell me why everyone around here acts like I am made of glass!"

"They don't think you are made of glass," I replied calmly. "They think you are made of ice."

- Mirror, mirror on the wall,
  Who's afraid of the great big fall?

- Leaders always have the
  opportunity to simply trust
  the process.

- I laugh a lot with my clients. However, my very best, absolutely *most* favorite clients usually make me howl!

- Leaders often need to lighten up, not tighten up!

- The best leaders know when to get out of their own way.

- Though our egos long for separate turfs, we need to learn to work in more integrative ways. Sometimes we have to remind ourselves that separation and pure functionalism generally lead to poor decision making.

- Wise leaders work hard to accomplish what they want to achieve within the context of understanding what they cannot control. In other words, they know when and how to push forward and when to let go without resorting to hopelessness or negative resignation.

- Wise leaders and mentors help other people unravel their power, ego, and control issues. Too many people have experiences of working with abusive supervisors or bosses who wield too much power. Overpowering leaders do not motivate people to reach their goals.

- When a leader is afraid to assert his or her power effectively he or she will be seen as irresponsible and ineffective. An astute leader will not be afraid to look at his or her relationship to power.

*W*ise leaders have exceptional
relationship and communication
skills. They find human connections
to be deeply satisfying.

*W*ise leaders have an astute understanding about people. They comprehend the universal behaviors that make all human beings tick. Wise leaders understand how to create ideas and solutions with other human beings. Wise leaders seek to enhance the ways in which people can harmoniously live, work, and create together. ∎

- Wise leaders have learned that building relationships is just as important as building products.

- Business issues are *always* people issues. Mature leaders never shy away from people issues. They realize that people *and* relationships have to be factored into any business problem. Weak band-aid approaches toward complex business issues are the result of immature leaders losing sight of the people issues involved in every business problem.

- Wise leaders have learned to invest the time and energy necessary to bring out the best in people. They know that the best solutions require the best use of human energy. Wise leaders do not see this type of leadership work as inconsequential to the task of leadership.

- Most leaders need to update their thinking about conflict. What if we didn't label conflict as "good" or "bad"? What if we simply viewed conflict as energy in motion? Energy can always be redirected. A mature leader views conflict like any stage of evolution—as an opportunity for growth. Seasoned leaders are always very skilled in conflict management.

- A seasoned leader knows the difference between a work group and a team. The act of simply labeling any corporate work group a team does not guarantee the use of any team behaviors. Using a team approach toward getting work done requires a substantial investment of time and energy. This investment can be well worth these efforts and expenditures. A mature leader knows how to cultivate a passion for teaming *and* how to build the skills necessary for utilizing team behaviors.

- In most agencies, there is a lot of talk about building partnerships. I suggest that leaders need to ask themselves this important question: "In building true partnerships, what power relationships are we *really* willing to create?"

- Just because we bring our people skills to work doesn't mean we practice good psychology.

- Often, less experienced leaders complain to me about the challenges they experience when attempting to handle difficult people. Sometimes they tell me, "I didn't get into this line of work because I wanted to work with difficult people!" A wise leader expects to deal with both difficult people and difficult situations.

- In the name of healthy scientific debate, we often put on our best egos, find our favorite corners of the argument, and proceed to do verbal warfare. Are these behaviors really all that productive? Mature leaders are not afraid to discuss opposing points of view. However, they view verbal warfare as counterproductive to real progress.

- Mature leaders can turn unhealthy debate into good dialogue because they know how to model the use of nondefensive communication.

- It takes a lot of energy and time to defend one's self. We forget how much time and energy we lose when we don't establish trusting relationships. High levels of trust and high levels of work productivity are directly correlated. Wise leaders insist that people build trusting relationships.

- What some leaders call a poor attitude is better described as a drastic misuse of energy.

- Excellent leaders know when to use a team approach toward getting work done and when to use a more functional or traditional approach.

- People are not usually impressed by gimmicks and slick sales techniques. Excellent leaders have learned that the "management by best-seller" approach seldom changes people's behavior.

- A seasoned leader will *never* hire anyone with poor people skills or a low level of emotional maturity—not for any job or for any reason. In fact, often a mature leader has learned this lesson the hard way.

■ Whenever we are in a relationship where there is a lack of trust, there is also a high degree of fear. Wise leaders are not afraid to talk about building trust in the workplace. They do not consider trust building initiatives to be a silly waste of time.

- Although we may not want to admit it, the relationships we have with ourselves mirror the relationships we have with those we lead. If we are relentlessly critical toward ourselves, we will be blaming and critical toward others.

- Wise leaders have learned to observe their own role in the relationship dances we all engage in so frequently. An astute leader can recognize his or her own dysfunctional dance steps.

- One day, my business partner, Daniel, noticed that he and I were using very different styles of managing conflict. The more Daniel would distance himself from any highly emotionally charged discussion, the more I would attempt to continue the discussion or even argue with Daniel. Our "chaser/distancer" conflict dance is a common one. When we stopped the dance, we were able to resolve our differences much more peacefully.

■ My friend Clare often reminds
me that beautiful relationships
aren't always pretty. All solid
relationships take a great deal of
hard work. Mature leaders work
at building relationships. They
hang in with people during
difficult times. They observe
their own relationship skills, and
they aim to build, rather than
devalue, the role of relationships
in work settings. 89

■ Every time we blame, we victimize. Every time we victimize, we blame. The blame/victimize game creates a vicious circle that generates a lot of contagious, negative energy in the working world. It is very counter-productive, and also very common in many of today's corporate environments. Solid leaders commit to reducing blame and victimizing in the work setting.

- Excellent leaders never assume that silence means agreement—especially when making critical team decisions.

- Wise leaders spend most of their careers learning more about the ways in which people do or do not relate well with each other. Wise leaders believe that we can build the types of relationships between human beings that will foster the development of a more sustainable and better world. Wise leaders are not afraid to hold this altruistic view.

Wise leaders lead with a strong sense of authenticity and integrity.

*W*ise leaders have a strong commitment to their personal value system, and they demonstrate this in the action steps they take when they lead. Their actions align with their core values. Wise leaders are highly committed, responsible human beings. They are not afraid to make very difficult decisions. ■

- Wise leaders appear authentic to others. They wear very few false masks. In fact, they know a lot about their own false masks and work hard to dismantle them. Their actions and their behaviors are congruous with their words and true feelings.

- Mature leaders create work cultures that tend to encourage people to take responsibility for the choices they make. These leaders hold themselves and others accountable for their behaviors and actions.

■ The most mature leaders I have worked with demonstrate a very high degree of emotional responsibility. They do not blame, shame, or victimize themselves or others. They are highly accountable to themselves and to others. They expect the same from the people with whom they work.

- You can write performance measurements for *anything* people do at work. Soft skills are highly measurable. Mature leaders hold people accountable for both hard-skill and soft-skill development.

- Everyone knew he was a poor performer—everyone except the attorney who read his squeaky clean performance folder.

- Ironically, in the name of having our "act together," we often appear as inauthentic, arrogant, and very controlling.

- I asked Ron what he thought had happened, and why he thought his people had turned on him. "Oh, I don't know," Ron responded. "I think I listened to some old-fashioned advice." "What advice was that?" I asked. "Oh, you know," Ron answered, "Never tell your people the whole truth."

- A wise leader never shelters his direct reports from the truth.

- The wisest leaders I have worked with are seldom afraid to utter the simple words: "I don't know."

- I asked Tom how he felt about not getting the position he had been promised. It was a position he wanted very badly. "Oh, I think Sue deserves it," Tom answered quickly. "She'll do a good job." "But how do you feel about not getting it yourself?" I pressed. "Sue will need my support, and I will give it to her," Tom continued. I knew Tom trusted me, so I pushed him one more time. "How do you really feel?" I asked for the third time. "Furious," Tom exploded, as he pounded his desk.

- It takes a tremendous amount of energy for any of us to mask our fears. Mature leaders work hard at creating the types of work environments that allow for real candor and honesty. A mature leader does not want people to be afraid to speak up in his or her presence. When people are not afraid they can do much more creative and productive work.

- If we are able to be honest with ourselves about the mistakes we have made (without being overly harsh or judgmental toward ourselves), we will be able to gather more wisdom.

- A mature leader doesn't act squeamish when asked to express his or her feelings openly.

- Although vulnerability is not welcomed in many corporate boardrooms, leaders who are not afraid to show their true feelings often garner the most respect and trust from others outside the boardroom.

- Dave justified promoting Bill, who was reputed to be a very verbally abusive supervisor, because Bill demonstrated so much technical competency. Dave and Bill *both* need coaching. Leaders who are unwilling to confront poor performers are demonstrating an equal measure of poor performance themselves.

- I encourage CEOs to take off their psychological masks and let go of their acts. It often takes a lot of deep psychological work to learn to let go of our idealized self-images. When we are able to finally do this, however, we offer authenticity and real power.

- Brian promised his direct reports an opportunity to take part in the executive-level bonus program in exchange for additional sales work. When it came time for Brian to negotiate for bonus moneys for his staff, he found a way to postpone his promise. Brian did this three times. Brian cannot understand why his people have become low performers. He does not know that all five of his key people have asked to be transferred out of his department.

- Dan told people he would hold them accountable for changes that needed to be made in his department. Dan's predecessor had said the same words but had not demonstrated a willingness to address poor performance. When Dan removed the non-performers from his department, people were shocked. Dan was criticized by some and congratulated by others. Dan did not react to any of this feedback; he simply stayed focused on his bottom line.

- Wise leaders have a strong commitment to their personal value system. They demonstrate this commitment by doing what they say they are going to do. It is as simple and as complicated as that.

- People constantly test new leaders to see if they are willing to "walk their talk." Perhaps learning to "walk our talk" is part of the way in which we gather wisdom.

Wise leaders demonstrate a high degree of emotional maturity.

Wise leaders have learned to tolerate the kinds of emotional upheaval that other people frequently find too difficult to handle. Wise leaders do not flee from difficult situations or difficult feelings. Wise leaders can handle chaotic or painful situations without needing to apply quick fix strategies or solutions. ■

- Wise leaders are familiar with their own psychological defenses and can recognize the psychological defenses used by others. They work hard at learning to lower their emotional reactivity as often as possible.

- All human beings have shadow sides and blind spots within their personalities. An excellent leader will not expect anyone to be perfect.

- Wise leaders work hard to accept their own imperfections without letting themselves off the hook for poor leadership behavior.

- Some of us confuse aging with maturing. Mature leaders have learned what it means to use grown-up behaviors.

- A mature person will remain responsible for all the choices he or she makes.

- As leaders mature, they learn to sit still when chaos, resistance, or difficult feelings are impacting their work. They learn how to remain calm without over-reacting, distancing, or detaching themselves too much from whatever is happening.

- We are never truly separate from our feelings. We just *think* we are. Wise leaders know the difference between expressing their thoughts and expressing their feelings.

- Many leaders are not skilled in the area of dealing with difficult feelings or charged emotions. Wise leaders learn to deal with all kinds of feelings.

- When we suppress, repress, or deny our feelings, we usually get ourselves into trouble. And when we confuse feeling our feelings with acting out, we get into another type of trouble. It takes a great deal of practice to learn to just feel our feelings without being driven by them. Mature leaders understand that learning to deal with difficult feelings is a lifelong practice.

- What if we stopped trying to create "feel good" work cultures? What if we stopped trying to eliminate "feel bad" work cultures? What if we simply allowed "feel what is real" work cultures?

- Anger usually covers pain, vulnerability, or fear. Mature leaders do not forget this basic rule of psychology.

- When someone drives you
  absolutely crazy, pushes all your
  buttons, and triggers every
  defense in your body, there is
  only one mature thing left to
  do . . . thank the universe for
  sending you your best teacher.

- Our goal as leaders is to become more emotionally whole. This means integrating and understanding *all* of the parts of ourselves, especially those parts we dislike, disown, and generally run away from. When we embrace and integrate the parts of our leadership style we are ashamed of, repress, or deny, we can transform our blindness into acceptance and creative energy.

- Mature leaders have learned to integrate (rather than bury) their psychological shadows. In the immature models of emotional growth, we attempt to cut out our bad parts. In the more mature models of growth, we can learn to integrate all parts of ourselves.

- Our old, unconscious family rules often shape our leadership behaviors. We do not need to reject or attempt to get rid of our family rules. Instead, we need to become aware of these rules so that we can make better choices about when and how to let them inform our decisions or direct our behaviors.

- The more mature the leader, the more willing he or she will be to honestly examine his or her behaviors.

- Any overly critical boss is a person who houses a very harsh inner critic. Usually, he or she has learned to use a series of harsh inner voices to whip himself or herself into performing exceptionally well. We need to remember that we are not our critical voice. Our critical voice is simply a series of thoughts that have formed into a well oiled psychological defense mechanism.

- Karen was a very good leader who was known for being relentlessly honest with her staff about her own weaknesses and shortcomings. Actually, she was like a warrior when it came to searching for her blind spots. I had to slow Karen down. In her attempts at being honest with herself, she was also developing a harshness toward herself. Slowly, I convinced Karen of the necessity of being compassionate toward herself while she examined what she considered to be her faults. As Karen softened toward herself, she integrated her weaknesses much more easily. This was a sign of emotional maturity.

- Most of us are terrified about accepting our humanness. We are afraid to see the ways in which we are not perfect. On the other hand, most of us are equally terrified about accepting our highest potential or our greatest gifts. This internal teeter-totter keeps us experiencing a great deal of frustration and a lot of emotional pain.

■ Emotional pain isn't as personal as many of us believe it to be. Pain was here before we were born on this planet, and it will be here after we leave. Mature leaders have learned how to deal wisely with emotional pain. They do not allow themselves to be seduced by excessive emotional drama, and yet they are not afraid to face real suffering.

- Bob (an excellent leader) values what I call "emotional maturity" and what he labels "psychological readiness" in people. He has asked the members of his executive leadership team do some personal psychological growth work within the next six months. Some of the team members are highly resistant. They don't want to venture into what they call "touchy feely" leadership development initiatives. Bob is not daunted by his team's resistance or nervousness. He wants to raise the emotional maturity in his top leadership team, and he plans to do whatever it takes to accomplish this objective.

- We all have resistance to feeling certain types of feelings. We tell ourselves that we should not feel angry or we should not feel giddy, or whatever. Our negative feelings about certain feelings stop us from integrating certain energies.

- As a leader, do you censor certain thoughts or feelings in yourself or others? Don't be afraid to examine this question thoroughly. Many leaders censor too many thoughts or feelings in themselves and others.

- Why do certain ideas, thoughts, or feelings cause you to react so strongly? A wise leader keeps examining his or her reactivity.

- "Tom pushes all of my buttons!" Lisa raged for what seemed like the tenth time during our two-hour coaching session. Lisa wasn't ready to look at her reactivity. She was, however, ready to look at Tom's behavior.

- Wise leaders know that no other person can really push their buttons—we allow our own buttons to be pushed by responding with too much reactivity. The more emotional maturity we gain, the easier it is to deal with emotional reactivity.

- If someone's critical remark reminds you of a voice of criticism from years ago, hit the emotional reactivity brake immediately. We are all much more reactive than we realize. Mature leaders are not afraid to look at who and what creates a lot of emotional reactivity for them.

- All of our self-loathing, judgment, and self-criticism weigh us down. This often manifests as real weight, body disease, or too much intensity. Some of our best performers suffer from chronic, unconscious self-loathing.

- Even great performance can be a defense mechanism.

- The decisions that we fight for and defend most adamantly are usually linked to both our greatest passions and our deepest sources of pain. Wise leaders examine what types of passions and pain fuel their most important decisions.

- A very wise leader can always tell the difference between real trauma and drama.

- Wise leaders are more comfortable than others with having to be uncomfortable.

*W*ise leaders aim to embrace balance in their lives.

Wise leaders realize that attaining physical, emotional, and spiritual balance in all aspects of their lives is a requirement for gathering more wisdom. They seek to renew themselves on a daily basis. Wise leaders develop practices for attaining balance in their lives and apply discipline in order to utilize these practices. ■

■ When we move toward
  wholeness, we start to relate
  to ourselves and others in ways
  that are more authentic, more
  satisfying, and more creative.
  Leaders need to think about
  the concept of wholeness. Can
  we create work environments
  where people can aim to become
  more whole? I am sure the
  answer is yes.

- Wise leaders value intelligence and wisdom equally. They simultaneously work at staying smart and growing more wise.

- Wise leaders do not need to make a deep separation between their personal lives and their business lives.

- Mature leaders have learned to value the present as well as the future and the past.

- The best leaders that I have worked with know that self-reflection is not a luxury, but a necessity.

- I often hear people in corporate America using the phrase, "My plate is too full." An excellent teacher once told me, "Pay very close attention to what you want to say yes to. Don't pay as much attention to what you need to say no to."

- Inexperienced leaders are often absolutely convinced that if they just drive themselves and everyone else much faster and much harder, they will accomplish much more. Even experienced leaders can fall into this trap, especially when they take on new and challenging leadership positions. These leaders do not realize how cold, brittle, and exhausted they appear. They do not comprehend what impact their overzealous style has on other peoples' behavior.

- I often ask leaders to memorize this line: "Too much strain results in very little gain."

■ The strategic planning retreat wasn't going well. People were angry, frustrated, and starting to attack each other verbally. "So, Linda," the CEO shouted from the back of the room, "we are paying you a lot of money to help us move forward. What's the most important thing we need to do this afternoon?" "Each person put your cell phone down and go walk on the beach alone for two hours," I quickly countered. The CEO immediately told everyone to follow my instructions. The rest of the meeting was very successful. Later, my business partner asked me why I had used such a nontraditional facilitating strategy. "I always trust silence," I responded.

- The new CEO asked me an important question during our first executive coaching session. "How can I nurture others, listen more openly, and be more effective without appearing too feminine?" he pondered. "Don't be afraid to use your less active and more receptive skills," I responded. "As a leader you need to hold both feminine and masculine energies," I continued. "We all do."

- The best team leaders I have worked with understand the importance of balancing content, relationship, and simple effective process in order to produce excellent services and products. Inexperienced leaders tend to overvalue content, undervalue or even devalue relationship, and over complicate process. This pattern creates organizational dysfunction as well as many other problems.

- Leaders who do too much, work too hard, and stay too busy often suffer from perfectionism. They are unaware of the strain they create for themselves and others. It is easy for them to convince themselves that they are just doing their job well, rather than face their impulse toward perfectionism. Almost all leaders must work their way through stages of perfectionism on the way to learning to lead effectively.

- When a leader tells me that he or she enjoys doing very little in life outside of his or her corporate work, I immediately look for signs of addictive behavior. We cannot contribute effectively when we are abusing ourselves.

- When leaders encourage, support, or model workaholism, they expose their organization to a great deal of risk.

- Lydia (a very well-paid executive) tried to convince me that she could handle working ten- and twelve-hour days for months at a time without losing her sense of corporate vision. During an executive coaching session she told me she had spent hours the week before obsessing about the choice of color for the new summer shirts she planned to give her sales staff. Lydia did not realize how much she had begun to focus on small, unimportant details. Her perspective was clouded by stress and fatigue.

- Wise leaders do not deny or hide from their exhaustion.

- Just because we have stopped talking doesn't mean we have silenced our minds.

- Wise leaders practice silencing their minds on a daily basis.

- Often we are so busy thinking that we can't hear our brilliance trying to come through.

- Perfectionism:
  Striving . . . Obsessive . . .
  Control oriented . . .
  Compulsive . . . Harsh . . .
  Straining . . . Driven . . .
  Insistent . . . Exhausting . . .
  Forcing!

- "When was the last time you were actually 'present in your body'?" my business partner asked me. "About a month ago," I replied honestly. A wise leader does not forget that he or she lives in a body that needs to be listened to all the time.

- If we all chose one day a week to really slow down, what would we be able to achieve or accomplish? The most mature leaders have found the balance point between activity and rest. Most of us need help finding that balance point.

- In a moment of honest self-observation Daniel noticed that he had blown his presentation because he was so distracted. In good humor, he announced, "Where am I when I really need me?" It is important for leaders to learn to be focused. Wise leaders often develop a practice or discipline for deep concentration.

- A strong, mature leader finds the courage to do some self-reflection once in a while. An excellent Buddhist teacher taught me to ask myself the following two questions as a way of reflecting:

"What is it I consistently avoid or run away from?"

"What is it I consistently cling to?"

- Wise leaders understand the need for time out, silence, and self-reflection in their lives.

Wise leaders are compassionate human beings.

*W*ise leaders work hard to bring out the best in themselves and other people. They inspire others to do the same. Wise leaders do not shy away from being viewed as fun loving, enthusiastic, caring, or even deeply loving human beings. Wise leaders understand how to care about people without aiming to take care of them. ■

- Paul, a leader I have known for many years, is highly respected and trusted by his coworkers. Paul works in a setting where people often feel overworked and very stressed. Paul's willingness to constantly try to bring out the best in people in this difficult environment speaks volumes about his strength and maturity as a leader. I once asked Paul why he seems to recognize so much good in people. "People," Paul told me, "mostly want to do their best. My job is to help them do just that."

- Wise leaders often have experienced enough difficult life experiences to have an acute understanding about the ways in which all human beings suffer. As wise leaders embrace learning more about human suffering, they are often more willing to make specific changes in their own lives as well as in the world around them.

- Spiritually mature leaders demonstrate a belief that people are much more alike than they are different. The wisest leaders demonstrate a sincere acceptance for diversity.

- Wise leaders sincerely care about other human beings. They are not afraid to demonstrate compassion, even when other people question their motives or poke fun at them for doing so.

- Wise leaders are often "meaning makers."

- As we seek more wisdom, we begin to understand that mastery can be an illusion.

- I teach a week-long seminar called, "The Leadership Intensive." Often when I teach this course, people tell me they are interested in developing their compassionate or spiritual leadership roles. If we believe that we are always connected to spirit, we can view all leadership as compassionate, spiritual leadership.

- Wise business leaders often embrace some form of deep spirituality in their lives. They do not, however, impose their spiritual views on others.

■ Twenty people stood comforting each other in the lobby of an office where I frequently work. They had just learned that their director's husband had died of cancer earlier in the day. Most of these people were not afraid to show their vulnerability. Their boss had demonstrated a strong sense of caring toward most of them for many years, and it was their turn to follow suit.

■ Remorse, instead of guilt.
Surrender, instead of resignation.
Wise spiritual leadership . . . you
get the picture.

■ I work for a man who is a fast-paced leader. He doesn't always take time to tend to relationships. After I learned that this man's son had recently left the states to fight in the war in Iraq, I told him I would keep his son in my thoughts. He responded by telling me he would also think about my young nephew, who had recently enlisted in the United States Marines. When we talked I could feel the sincere compassion in his voice and it moved me deeply.

- Wise leaders embrace focus, direction, and mastery in their lives. They also embrace confusion, paradox, and mystery.

- When there is a continued absence of caring in any organization, we can expect fear, apprehension, anger, anxiety, bitterness, hopelessness, and despair to be the prevailing emotions.

- So many of the less mature leaders I have worked with are really nervous about being seen as compassionate leaders. They tell me they worry about being seen as too caring. These leaders have not entered the path of wise leadership.

- Any leader who uses shame or fear as a tool for manipulation helps fuel a vicious cycle of hopelessness and rage in those he or she leads.

■ I recently witnessed a group of
leaders from a large federal agency
spending tremendous amounts of
time, energy, and even personal
money helping a young coworker
do battle with pancreatic cancer.
The amount of compassion these
coworkers demonstrated reminded
me of how resilient people can be
in the face of real suffering. I had
an opportunity to talk with the
young woman right before she
died. She told me she considered
it a privilege to find her way
toward her own death with the
help of such fine people. I cried
when she told me that. I know the
people she was talking about—
they are all big-hearted leaders.

- I recently had the opportunity to work with a woman who had experienced a lot of personal suffering during the preceding year. When I met her she had just been placed in charge of a large leadership initiative. I watched how she approached each daunting task with a sense of trust in the people around her. She remained focused and calm. Her predecessor (a woman I knew quite well) had approached the same tasks with a very negative attitude. I found her to be brittle and cold toward people. It was striking to feel the difference in the two leaders' use of energy.

- Ryan considers himself to be a very caring leader. He worries constantly about helping his coworkers, and he spends a great deal of time helping them achieve their goals. Behind closed doors, however, Ryan complains bitterly about the amount of time and energy he has to expend in order to help others. Ryan still has a desire to be *seen* as a kind, helpful, and positive leader.

  Ryan is gathering more wisdom about his mask. He is beginning to feel the difference between helping someone else in order to feel good about himself and truly helping without any attachment to how people view him.

■ One of the wisest women I have worked for models true compassionate leadership very well. She cares about herself enough to take the time to do the things she needs to do in order to keep herself in physical, emotional, and spiritual balance. By doing this she is able to stay connected to others in a way that is extraordinary. This woman accomplishes a great deal in the world. She cares deeply about herself and others.

- Wise leaders do not confuse caring about people with promoting entitlement-oriented work cultures.

- A mature leader understands the fine line between codependency and compassion.

- Wisdom and leadership often are linked to age and maturity. I also find wisdom and leadership to be linked to the depth of a person's heart.

- Wise leaders seek out as many questions as they do answers.

- The wisest leaders embrace everything.

PRINCIPLES OF EVOLVED LEADERSHIP

■ Leadership that values the development of intellectual capacity in the individual as well as development of wisdom in the individual.

■ Leadership that seeks and expects continuous growth —even when growth is extremely uncomfortable and painful.

■ Leadership that demands personal accountability and personal responsibility for one's self at all times.

■ Leadership that recognizes, accepts, and manages vulnerability in humans and human systems.

■ Leadership that recognizes, accepts, and manages diversity in humans and human systems.

■ Leadership that embraces change for what it really is— a difficult process of letting go of the old, with a resultant stage of chaos that precedes movement toward the unknown.

■ Leadership that embraces focus, direction, and mastery as well as ambiguity, paradox, and mystery.

■ Leadership that engages in the constant pursuit of creativity, competency, congruency, and compassion.

APPENDIX

THE WAY WE BRING CLOSURE TO OUR UNFULFILLED leadership dreams is important. Many of the best leaders I have worked with have suffered when they have not been able to accomplish something that was of great importance either to themselves or others. I have learned a lot by watching the wisest leaders handle their suffering and their losses. The wisest seem to do this with both a sense of grace and a sense of gratitude for having had a chance to be in the leadership game in the first place. I have a deep respect for those hard-working leaders who handle their suffering and their losses with a great deal of maturity.

The wisest leaders seem to embrace their losses by entering their disappointments fully. They do this without denying or repressing their hurt and angry feelings. Although they allow themselves to feel their most challenging emotions, they do not become overly dramatic or bitter in their quest to acknowledge what often amounts to real loss and grief. They do not take their disappointments out on others, and they do not stay stuck in the blame/victim game. They honestly admit how difficult it is to let go, and then they summon the courage to move toward accomplishing newer visions. Wise leaders often seem to let go with a sense of grace. They seem to have a deep trust in the universe, and this trust allows them to put their goals to rest when they most need to let go of the insistence that things go their own way. Interestingly enough, once they really let go of their expectations, they often manifest their original visions in forms that are different from, yet very similar to, their original ideas. It is exciting to be able to observe this delicate and important process.

One of my favorite clients is an avid bicyclist. When he is not working, he often takes part in long and arduous bicycle trips. He has a strong sense of determination, a wonderful sense of humor, and a great deal of tenacity. Although he has accomplished a lot in his long career, in all likelihood he will end it knowing he has not been able to attain one of his final leadership goals. I am sure he will retire with a mild sense of disappointment, but also with a sense of serenity. This man is a very wise leader, and he has prepared himself for a personal loss of sorts. His mind is clear, and his heart is open. He is ready to retire and enter the next phase of his life knowing that he has done his best in his role as a leader. I know he will continue to accomplish many important things in the world.

The following is an excerpt from a letter I wrote to him about one year prior to his expected retirement. At the time of this writing, he was anguishing over his decision to retire.

■ ■ ■

Dear Don,

I observed you struggling a lot in our last executive retreat. After returning from the retreat I decided to take the risk to write you the following letter. Please forgive me for being the "advice giver" on this occasion. I hope you will hear me offering you words of support as you continue to wrestle with your decision about when and how to retire.

As you know, sometimes our most important leadership dreams fall apart or come to an end before we are completely ready to let them go. It seems like the things we most want to accomplish or do in life don't always manifest on our own terms. The universe doesn't always seem to want to cooperate with us exactly the way we would like it to, and suddenly we are stuck with all that loss. At times like these all of our most challenging and difficult emotions can kick into first gear. In keeping with your strongest life metaphor, I will refer to these challenging times as "the times we break our favorite bikes." I would like to share with you what I have learned from others (as well from my own life experiences) about handling these times. I know you will follow my bicycle metaphor.

When our favorite bike breaks down and we know we need to put it away for good, we can create a lot of chaos for ourselves. If we throw our broken bike down on the sidewalk in utter frustration and then try to walk away too fast without mourning our loss, we tend to carry a bent wheel or blown bike tire around with us for a long time. The problem with this strategy is that we can't see the broken bike parts hanging off ourselves. We sit in some meeting throwing around a bike part or two and don't understand why people are irritated by our behavior.

Contrary to this strategy, sometimes we get off our broken bike and sit next to it in the road for way too long a period of a time. We love our old bike, and it just about kills us to have to let it go, even when it is completely broken. We find ourselves talking about our bike too much of the time, bringing out the old bike pictures way too often. We even catch ourselves buying new bike fenders in the same color as our old ones just to remind us of what we lost. Unfortunately, people can't hang around listening to us forever while we stay too connected to our unfulfilled passions. Even the most supportive people in our lives begin to get edgy with us when we can't seem to put our lost dreams to rest. Eventually they stop listening to us, and at a certain point they even get up and walk away, leaving us alone to face our disappointments.

It's difficult to learn to let go of our lost leadership dreams in a skillful and graceful manner. It takes time and maturity to know exactly when and how to put something important to rest. However, with lots of practice (and a few big crashes along the way), most of us can learn to let go of what we thought we most needed to accomplish, attain, do, or even "be" in the world.

In a nutshell, sometimes we must let go of our leadership dreams, mourn the losses fully, and then move on to new things. Having said that, anyone can preach about learning to let go skillfully. Actually having to do it, however, often is the most painful thing a wise leader has to do in his or her career.

I find that it helps tremendously to know that each one of us has a resiliency inside ourselves that is much stronger than our lost dreams or broken bikes. When we really believe this, we begin to find out that resiliency is one of our best human attributes. Over the years I have watched you bounce back from disappointment many times. At this challenging juncture in your life, I want to remind you how resilient you are.

By the way, I almost forgot to mention that once we learn to let go of our old bike, we often get to ride a brand-new bike, if we really want to. It may not be the bike we wanted in the first place, and it will definitely not be the bike we miss, but there is a new bike out there for all of us. In the end, our new bikes will break just like our old ones did. That's okay, someday we might begin to learn to cherish the bike rides as much as the bikes themselves.

I wish you happy pedaling Don. You have taught me a tremendous amount about wise leadership. Thank you for being on both the giving and receiving end of our joint learning. I cherish the wonderful years we have spent working together.

Many Blessings,

LINDA

ABOUT THE AUTHOR

LINDA MCLYMAN is one of the principal partners in the executive management firm Progress Associates. If you are interested in attending an advanced leadership training program or would like to book Linda or her partner, Daniel Leete, for a speaking engagement, seminar, or executive coaching services she can be reached at: Progress Associates, 3827 Makyes Road, Syracuse, NY 13215; tel (315) 498-5599; *www.progressassociates.com.*